Bad Kids

Tony Robinson

Illustrated by Mike Phillips

Macmillan Children's Books

First published 2009 by Macmillan Children's Books
a division of Macmillan Publishers Limited
20 New Wharf Road, London N1 9RR
Basingstoke and Oxford
www.panmacmillan.com

Associated companies throughout the world

ISBN 978-0-230-73787-7

Text copyright © Tony Robinson 2009
Illustrations copyright © Mike Phillips 2009

1 3 5 7 9 8 6 4 2

A CIP catalogue record for this book is available from
the British Library.

Typeset by Dan Newman/Perfect Bound Ltd
Printed in China

My friend Jo Foster did a lot of the work involved in writing this book. She wants me to tell you that all the good jokes are hers, and the bad jokes are mine.

She may be a brilliant researcher, but in this instance she's totally, hopelessly wrong!

The Publisher would like to thank the following for permission
to reproduce their material. Every care has been taken to trace
copyright holders. However, if there have been unintentional
omissions or failure to trace copyright holders, we apologize and will,
if informed, endeavour to make corrections in any future edition.

Top = t; Bottom = b; Centre = c; Left = l; Right = r

Page 5 Art Archive/Dagli Orti; 6 Art Archive/Musée du Louvre Paris/Gianni Dagli Orti; 16 Art
Archive/Bodleian Library Oxford; 13 Art Archive/Dagli Orti; 19 Art Archive/National Museum Beirut/
Dagli Orti; 24 Art Archive/Bibliothèque des Arts Décoratifs Paris/Dagli Orti; 31 Art Archive/British
Library; 33l Alamy/Mary Evans Picture Library; 36 Art Archive/British Library; 38 Art Archive/Reading
Museum/Eileen Tweedy; 41 Alamy/Lebrecht Music and Arts Photo Library; 43 City of Bristol Record
Office; 44t Art Archive/Eglise Notre Dame Sémur en Auxois/Dagli Orti; 45 Art Archive/Musée Condé
Chantilly/Dagli Orti; 47 Art Archive/Bibliothèque Municipale Castres/Gianni Dagli Orti; 50 Art Archive/
University Library Heidelberg/Dagli Orti; 52 Art Archive/Bodleian Library Oxford; 53 Art Archive; 55 Art
Archive/Musée du Louvre Paris/Dagli Orti; 56 Alamy/Pictorial Press Ltd; 63 Alamy/Mary Evans Picture
Library; 68 Alamy/Mary Evans Picture Library; 69 Art Archive/Château de Blois/Gianni Dagli Orti; 70t
Art Archive; 71 Art Archive/Culver Pictures; 73 Art Archive; 74 Alamy/Mary Evans Picture Library; 78
Codex_Mendoza_folio_60r; 83 Art Archive; 84cr Alamy/IMAGEPAST; 84b The Chief Constable of the
Avon & Somerset Constabulary; 87t Getty/Hulton Archive; 87b Art Archive; 88 Alamy/Mary Evans Picture
Library; 89t Alamy/Mary Evans Picture Library; 92cr Alamy/The Print Collector; 93r Alamy/The Print
Collector; 94 Mary Evans Picture Library; 106 Corbis/Hulton; 107 Corbis/Hulton; 108 Corbis/Bettmann;
115 Mary Evans Picture Library; 116 Getty/Popperfoto; 117t Getty/Terrence Spencer/Time Life Pic; 117b
Getty/Hulton; 118t Getty/Hulton; 118b Getty/Stuart Nicol; 119 Getty/Ian Cook/Time Life Pictures; 120
Getty/Gilles Mingasson; 123 Getty/Lihee Avidan; 124 Getty/Matt Cardy; 128 Getty/Chris Hondros; 129
Alamy/Lisa Ryder

Contents

Serious Warning!!!

When you were little and a bit of a bad kid, did your mum ever tell you that if you didn't stop drawing on the wallpaper with your felt-tip pen, a green hairy monster would come and get you?

Well, you're not alone.

All over the world, grown-ups try to scare kids witless so they'll behave.

In Spain, mums and dads tell their children there's a horrible bogeyman called 'El Coco', who hides under the bed and pops out to eat bad kids.

In ancient Greece, there was supposed to be an evil demon called Mormo, who sank her fangs into kids who misbehaved.

And the Zuni Indians in the USA said there was an old monster man and an old monster woman, who carried a basket and a hook so they could catch bad kids and gobble them up.

Are you getting a bit jumpy?

Then you'd better stop reading this book immediately.

I mean it.

Tear it in two, give it away to Oxfam, or sell it and buy a load of sweets.

Spanish goblins under the bed, Mormo and her child-chomping teeth, the old monster couple and their horrible hook are nothing compared to the disgusting, real-life punishments that have been used to frighten kids into being good since the days when your ancestors wandered around in suits made of mammoth hair.

Still reading? This is your last chance. If you don't want to hear about some REALLY nasty stuff . . .

WALK AWAY FROM THIS BOOK –
RIGHT NOW!!!!!!!!!!!

Right. All the wimps have gone — let's get down to business. What were these horrible punishments?

How about if your teacher beat you up with a big stick . . .

. . . if your dad burned you with a red-hot lump of metal . . .

. . . if he held you over burning chilli peppers until your eyes and windpipe were stinging . . .

. . . and if you got your fingers cut off, or were sold into slavery, or sat in chains on a mouldy boat for six months and were taken to the other side of the world, where you would never see your family again?

Forget monsters; this stuff is for real!

You're about to read about *horrible crimes,*

horrible punishments

and some very horrible kids!

Bad kids haven't changed much over the years. You may spot this bunch again . . .

Chapter 1

Pyramids, gladiators and skewering

Which explains why naughty boys couldn't pick their noses!

More than five thousand years ago, when the rest of us were running around in animal skins clobbering antelope with big clubs . . .

. . . the people of southern Iraq had a very nice lifestyle.

How come?

Because they lived in cities – with plenty of food, proper houses, nice furniture and indoor bathrooms . . . in fact they practically invented cities. Most other people lived in caves, in huts and in villages.

Big cities are exciting, fast-moving places. There's lots of money about, loads of shops, and people come to them from far away

with strange new music, weird accents and crazy ideas like building toilets instead of squatting over holes in the ground.

The trouble is that cities get crowded – and you know what it's like if you have to share a small bedroom with your brother or sister, or you're stuck in a crowded school bus in a traffic jam. Voices get raised, rows start and fists fly. The same was true of the first cities; they could easily turn into pretty lawless places.

A very long list of dos and don'ts in ancient Iraq

So the Iraqis invented writing. And what did they use this brand-new invention for?

To create the world's first football league tables?

No.

To scribble down a nice little recipe for fresh strawberry mousse wrapped in chocolate with a cream topping?

No.

They made up laws telling the people in the big cities not to muck about, and wrote them down.

One of these laws said that if a father told his son, 'You're not my son,' the son had to leave home and give up everything he owned. This might not seem very fair, although it would have been a bit fairer if the son had been allowed to say the same thing to his

3

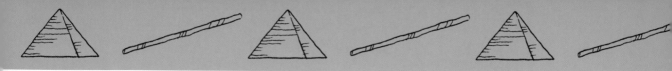

father. But he wasn't, because if the words 'You're not my father' even sneaked out of the corner of his mouth his dad was allowed to cut his hair off and sell him as a slave!

In fact, if you were a dad and your son misbehaved, you could do all kinds of nasty things to him, like lock him up and put heavy chains around his ankles. You could even take a red-hot branding iron out of the fire and press it against his forehead until it sizzled and left a permanent scar.

COULD YOU GO BACK? I THINK I'VE MISSED ONE!

But they didn't have newspapers, televisions or the Internet in those days, so how did ordinary people know what was allowed and what wasn't?

Because the great Iraqi King Hammurabi had all the laws chiselled on to **huge stones** so everyone in his cities could see them.

So, for instance, if you were walking down the high street and you glanced up at the massive stones, you might notice Hammurabi's Law number 195, which said, 'If a son hits his father, his fingers shall be cut off.'

And from that moment on you'd know that if you ever clouted your dad, you could say goodbye to nose-picking.

4

Ancient Egypt

Around the corner from Iraq, another bunch of people were soon writing down their laws and punishments. I'm pretty sure you'll have heard of this lot: they're the ancient Egyptians.

Just like in Iraq, Egyptian fathers were allowed to clobber their kids (and their wives!) as much as they liked, and no one could stop them. Not only that, but teachers could whack kids too. This was thought pretty useful at the time, as it meant anyone could identify young troublemakers because they'd be covered in bruises.

One common punishment for pesky Egyptian kids was to put them in **the stocks**. These were wooden blocks with holes for their feet to keep the little terrors in one place so they couldn't run away when people came to jeer at them. I think I'd rather be given an ASBO, wouldn't you?

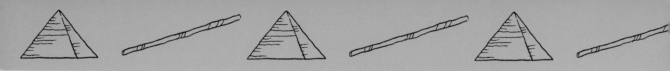

But that was nothing compared with what happened to you if your dad was a soldier and he ran away from the army. Then your whole family would be thrown in prison, and you'd have to stay there for weeks or months or even years till he came back.

Yes, Egyptian law-makers could be pretty tough!

An Egyptian happy family all hoping Dad doesn't do anything illegal

 This is what they did to your dad
if he stole an animal from the temple:

How to Skewer an Ancient Egyptian Criminal

1 *Take a long, sharpened bit of wood. Make sure it's nice and sturdy, with a decent point at one end.*

2 *Bury the blunt end in the ground firmly. Make sure it doesn't wiggle around.*

3 *Hold the prisoner up so his belly button is over the point. Then drop him quickly so the stick goes all the way through and out the other side.*

4 *Leave for several days, or until everyone's had a good look. Don't worry if he doesn't die straight away. That's perfectly normal.*

If seeing this happen to your dad wasn't bad enough, you and your entire family would then be handed over to the temple to work as slaves for the rest of your lives.

Ancient Israel

There's one book of ancient laws that still gets used around the world today. A poor little tribe called the Hebrews, who lived somewhere between Iraq and Egypt, put this book together. You've probably heard of it – it's called **the Bible**, and you might think it's all kind and gentle, full of commandments like 'Thou shalt not kill' and 'Love thy neighbour'. But bits of the Bible have plenty to say on the subject of how you should punish children, and the main message is hit them and don't hold back! Take these quotes from the Book of Proverbs, for instance:

This holy book may look pretty, but it's still full of rules!

'Foolishness is bound in the heart of a child; but the rod of correction shall drive it far from him.'

(In other words, 'Children are thick, but you can make them less stupid by clobbering them!')

'Withhold not correction from the child; for if thou beatest him with the rod, he shall not die. Thou shalt beat him with the rod, and shalt deliver his soul from hell.'

(Which means, 'Go ahead and whack your little darling – you're actually doing him a favour!')

Even if your dad did want you to die, that was OK too. This is what the Book of Deuteronomy says about stroppy kids: if you have a son who's a bit of a rebel and he ignores you when you tell him off, all the men of the city can throw rocks at him until he's dead.

And it doesn't even say he has to be given a fair trial first!

There was one piece of good news in Deuteronomy though: it said that 'the father shall not be put to death for the children, neither shall the children be put to death for the father'. In other words, Hebrew kids couldn't be punished for something their dads had done, unlike the poor old Egyptians.

IT WAS HIM!

THANKS A BUNCH, SON

Ancient Greece

The ancient Greeks thought they were pretty hot on justice and on things being fair. They were very proud of the fact that everybody had a say in all big decisions – absolutely everybody!

Well, **almost** everybody. Actually, it was everybody except the **slaves**.

So apart from slaves, everybody . . . except **poor people**.

So apart from poor people, everybody . . . except **women**.

Oh yes, and apart from the women and slaves and poor people, the **children** definitely didn't.

But what does being a child mean? How old did you have to be before you stopped being one? These days in the UK, the law says you are an adult when you become eighteen. That's when you get to vote, marry without your parents' permission, drink and smoke.

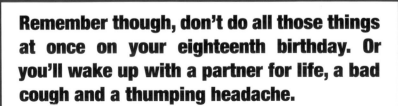

TELL ME ABOUT IT!

> **Remember though, don't do all those things at once on your eighteenth birthday. Or you'll wake up with a partner for life, a bad cough and a thumping headache.**

The ancient Greeks did things differently. They didn't know when someone was eighteen, because **birthdays** hadn't been invented yet.

When a Greek boy looked and acted as though he was seventeen or eighteen-ish, he became a man. But if he had a baby face or kept doing daft things, he'd have to wait until he was rather more sensible – a bit like being kept back a year in school. Once he was a man, he could vote, make a will, join the army, appear in court, and sign official papers.

A Greek girl didn't become a woman till she got married. After that, could she vote, join the army, and do all the other things her brother could do? No, but she was allowed to stay indoors a lot and do what her husband told her. Lucky her!

As a schoolboy in ancient Greece you were supposed to learn reading, writing and music, but, most importantly, you had to be brave. Teachers toughened up their pupils by hitting them whenever they stepped out of line. In fact the word for 'teach' in Greek is the same as the word for 'whack with a big stick'.

Bad Kid no. 1
Herakles

The Greeks' favourite superhero was called Herakles. His other name, the one the Romans used, was Hercules. He had amazing strength, even as a baby. Someone once put two poisonous snakes into his cot, and he strangled them both with his tiny little baby hands.

Later, when he was at school, his teacher Linus tried to teach

him to play the harp. But even though he had mighty powers, Herakles was tone-deaf. His music sounded like a room full of cats throwing up, and it drove his teacher so mad that he decided to wallop Herakles, but his pupil was having none of it. Instead Herakles jumped up, wrapped the harp round his teacher's head, and left him dead on the floor surrounded by bits of broken musical instrument.

Herakles was punished by being sent away to guard a herd of cows on a lion-infested mountain. But being a superhero, he managed to strangle the lion and skin it, and then used the fur as a smart new coat. It only took him a few minutes. Certainly beats the bother of trudging round the shops!

Occasionally, real-life Greek children 'did a Herakles', and took revenge on the adults who were mean to them. Slaves had very tough lives. It's not surprising that lots of them hated their masters, although mostly they were too scared to do anything about it.

But one eleven-year-old slave boy did. He decided he'd had enough, drew his knife, and tried to stab his master to death. But like all kids who use knives, he was dumb. The master yelled, the boy ran away, and the knife was left sticking in his master's body. When other people came rushing to see what all the fuss was about, it was obvious who'd done the stabbing, and the boy was put to death.

I imagine the other slaves would have felt very sorry for him, but it would also have been a big relief to them that the boy hadn't managed to finish their master off. If a slave did kill his boss, the law said that all the dead man's slaves should be executed.

Macho Spartan helmet!

In one part of Greece called Sparta, adults went out of their way to make life particularly difficult for their kids. Right from the start, Spartan children had to get used to a life that must have felt like one long punishment, specially designed to toughen them up.

When a baby was born its father took it to the local elders, whose job was to decide if it was healthy enough to grow up to be a proper Spartan. Any babies who were weak or disabled, and who the elders didn't think would make good soldiers, were thrown into a deep pit, miles from the city. In other parts of Greece, babies were often left on hillsides to die – but at least they'd have half a chance of being picked up by a passing hiker on a ramble. If a Spartan baby was thrown into a pit, they'd pretty much had it.

It's a daft thing to have done, I reckon. Some of those kids could have grown up to be great inventors, or clever generals, or even Paralympian athletes. The Spartans may have been tough, but they were a bit dumb.

Every Spartan boy had one aim: to be the best soldier around. Seven-year-old boys were sent away from home to start training. They weren't taught to read and write, just to be as tough as possible. They weren't given enough food or warm clothes, even in winter. They slept on itchy straw until they were fourteen and after that on rushes, which were even spikier. They even had to wade into ice-cold rivers to collect the rushes for themselves.

I DON'T KNOW BUT I'VE BEEN TOLD, RUSHES ARE SPIKY AND THE WATER'S COLD...

Once they were twelve and had a few years' training under their belts, they were taken to the front door of the temple of the goddess Artemis for their reward. At the other end of the temple was an altar covered in tasty cheeses and, as you can imagine, after years without a decent breakfast the boys would have been starving. But before they could sink their teeth into the delicious, squidgy cheese, they had to get past a bunch of mean men with whips, who didn't hold back and sometimes killed the boys. I think I'd have asked for a bowl of cornflakes instead.

Yes, Spartans definitely did things differently. Spartan kids were actually encouraged to steal stuff. The idea was that when they grew up and fought wars in foreign countries they'd be able to nick themselves some dinner. No one minded if you stole something – but there was hell to pay if you got caught.

There's a story of a Spartan boy who stole a fox, hid it under his cloak, and took it to school. When it started to nibble at his belly button, he kept quiet rather than squeal, and continued doing his sums until the fox gnawed out his guts and he fell off his chair, dead.

Ancient Italy

Over in Italy, the ancient Romans were crazy about the law, absolutely obsessed with it, and had rules for pretty much everything, including plenty for child criminals.

Generally, if you were under seven, you'd be OK. Under-sevens were considered too babyish to understand right from wrong, so they couldn't be found guilty. It was also illegal to torture kids younger than fourteen. Even young adults got given lighter punishments, because people weren't seen as properly grown-up until they were twenty-five.

BUT I'M ONLY SIX, HONEST, GUV

In some special cases those rules didn't apply. There was a very powerful man in Rome named Sejanus, who was great mates with the Emperor Tiberius. Tiberius made Sejanus head of his personal bodyguard, and let him employ more and more soldiers. Soon Sejanus got so big for his boots he started getting rid of anyone who got in his way, until eventually he was pretty much running the whole Roman Empire. He was absolutely ruthless. Some people think he even murdered the emperor's son, Drusus.

Eventually Tiberius had Sejanus arrested and killed, and who can blame him? But that was just the start. He then had Sejanus's **wife** killed . . .

followed by his **eldest son** . . .

which just left his two youngest **kids**, a boy and a girl.

They were put on trial too, even though officially they were too young to be found guilty. It seems pretty unjust to us, doesn't it? They hadn't done anything wrong; it was their grandad who was the criminal. But they were strangled anyway, and then thrown down a flight of steps.

Usually Roman kids needed to worry much more about their dads than about what anyone else might do to them. When a Roman baby was born, it was put on the floor at its father's feet. It was then up to Daddy to decide whether to look after it (in which case he'd pick it up and give it a cuddle) or ignore it. If he left it where it was, the baby would be taken out and put in a public place, where it might die or be carried off by a stranger.

The oldest man in a Roman family could do what he liked with his wife, his slaves, his kids and anyone else who lived in his house.

Even after he'd decided to look after a child, he was still allowed to . . .

disown it . . .

kill it . . .

or sell it into slavery.

That way, he could make a bit of cash as well as get one of his kids out from under his feet. He could also sell his kid for a while and then buy it back again. But after a child had been sold three times, it would be officially free. And pretty glad to see the back of its dad, I should imagine.

Just because they had lots of rules, it didn't mean the Romans were uptight goody-two-shoeses. In their spare time they enjoyed extreme sports like chariot racing and hunting wild beasts. And they loved watching gladiators tear each other to bits.

Gladiator fights didn't have an 18 certificate. Kids could go along too, and see people get chopped to bits with swords or eaten by lions. Just think how modern grown-ups worry

about whether computer games will turn their children into violent morons! If that's true, how much more head-bangingly ferocious must Roman children have been?

For a while there was a trend for Roman boys to travel to Greece to go to school. Whole groups of them would hang around with their new teacher in a little gang. The more pupils a teacher had the more important he was considered to be, so the boys would go out and kidnap other kids and make them join their class. Every time a boat full of eager new students came ashore, there'd be gangs of boys waiting to grab them, armed with knives, clubs and stones.

A teenager called Libanius heard about these fights and thought they sounded dead glamorous. He went to Athens to join in the kidnapping, but got kidnapped himself as soon as he got there – and was then kidnapped from his kidnappers by different kidnappers the very next day!

Nero getting ready
for a night out

Nero is famous for being a particularly evil and mad Roman emperor. He had some wild, antisocial ideas about how to have a good time. When he was nineteen, he went through a phase of getting drunk and running through the streets at night, but then a lot of young royals do that sort of thing, don't they? Unlike most modern royals though, he also enjoyed beating up passers-by. Two of his favourite hobbies were throwing people into sewers and bundling them up in blankets and giving them an extreme form of the birthday bumps. But one night, he went too far. He attacked a senator's wife, and the senator caught him and beat him black and blue without realizing who he was.

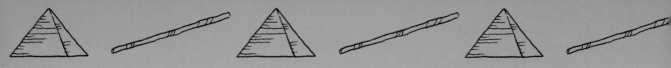

That might have taught a normal teenager a lesson, but Nero was emperor, so he could do whatever he liked. Soon after the ruckus, the senator found out who he'd been fighting with. He wrote to Nero straight away to say sorry. This was very stupid of him. Nero knew he'd been recognized, and didn't want anyone to know he'd lost the fight, so he made the senator kill himself. After that the emperor merrily carried on as before – only from then on he took a group of 'heavies' along with him so he'd win every punch-up.

For the Romans, being a Christian was a crime. If you didn't worship the Roman gods, you were for it. And being young didn't always save you. Take young Agapetus, for instance. Agapetus was a fifteen-year-old Christian who got into trouble for refusing to make a sacrifice to the gods. The Romans decided to make an example of him, and thought up some really nasty punishments. First they whipped him. Then they hung him upside down by his feet and poured boiling water all over him. Then they let wild beasts loose on him for a bit of a nibble. Lastly, just in case he hadn't got the message, they cut his head off.

> Yes, I know, it's not fair – and poor old Agapetus would probably agree. But then, life wasn't very fair in ancient times.

What Happened When

From 3500 BC — In ancient Iraq (also called Mesopotamia) people start living together in cities.

3000 BC — The clever Sumerians in Mesopotamia start writing things down – other Sumerians have to learn to read pretty quickly.

2500 BC — Great Pharaohs of Egypt build the Pyramids at Giza and the mysterious Sphinx.

1792 BC — Hammurabi becomes King of most of Mesopotamia.

1300 BC — Pharaoh Seti I gets tough on temple thieves – and their unlucky kids.

600 BC (ish) — Some of the laws of ancient Israel get written down in the Book of Deuteronomy. Rebellious kids have to start dodging rocks.

500 BC (ish) — Cities in ancient Greece become the new capitals of culture – and the people of Athens invent democracy (but not for kids).

404 BC — The super-tough Spartans beat the namby-pamby Athenians in a war. And probably steal all their stuff, just like they were taught to.

49–44 BC — Julius Caesar is the ruler of Rome, until he's murdered (as far as we know, no kids were involved).

AD 31 — Roman emperor Tiberius bumps off his uppity pal Sejanus – and just for good measure, Sejanus's kids too.

AD 56 — Teen emperor Nero goes through a nasty phase of beating people up in the street.

AD 336 — Libanius has the worst ever first day at school, getting kidnapped twice by his classmates.

Chapter 2

Castles, monks and beheading

Which includes a description of the ordeal by hot water

(No, it's not a nice warm bath with bubbles and a little plastic duck. It's something *much* more disgusting!)

People the world over make the same mistake – they think their civilization is the best there has ever been and it will go on forever.

But things don't work that way. Eventually all civilizations come to an end.

Nutters on horseback invade your country and slaughter you, or the world gets hotter and your rivers run dry, or it gets colder and your crops die. Something like that happened to ancient Egypt, ancient Israel and ancient Greece, and some day it will happen to us!

Even the mighty Roman Empire, which stretched from England to Syria, got too big, and its inhabitants got fat and lazy, and one thing led to another, and finally waves of hairy sword-waving Germans moved in and there was nothing the Romans could do to stop them.

When the Roman army left England our laws changed in a big way. For a start we were immediately invaded again, and the newcomers – the Jutes, the Saxons and the Angles – didn't give a stuff about Roman law. As far as they were concerned, if someone burned your house down, you could burn down theirs. If they chopped your arm off, you could chop off theirs, and if they killed your dad, they'd better look out because you'd be coming after them with a very sharp weapon!

Now this might sound fairly fair in a bullying, biggest-boy-in-the-playground sort of way, but there was a problem. Revenge can cause an awful lot of aggravation – even for innocent little kids who didn't have anything to do with the original argument.

For instance, there was this bloke called Utred, who fancied a girl and wanted to marry her, but her dad said he'd only agree if Utred first killed his arch-enemy, Thurbrand.

Thurbrand got to hear about it though, and as he didn't want to end up dead he killed Utred instead . . . plus forty of his followers.

But Utred had a son who was absolutely furious that his dad had been killed, so he slaughtered Thurbrand.

And Thurbrand's son murdered Utred's son.

And not to be outdone, Utred's family murdered Thurbrand's grandchildren and his great-grandchildren, who weren't even around when the carnage first started.

Saxons doing their slaughtering stuff

That's the trouble with revenge – it has a tendency to go on and on, even after people have forgotten what the original argument was all about.

With this kind of slaughter happening all over the country, it must have seemed as though soon there'd be no one left alive.

So the Saxons, who eventually took charge of most of southern England, came up with a neat solution. They decided that if somebody killed his neighbour, the local lord would decide how important the dead neighbour had been, then make the murderer pay money to the neighbour's family, and that would be the end of the matter. It might not be justice as we know it, but at least it stopped the endless killing.

Paying the Price for Murder

Our neighbours across the English Channel did pretty much the same thing. The Franks were a powerful tribe, who gave their name to the country of France. They had a price-list called the **Wergild**, which told you exactly how much you'd have to cough up if you bumped someone off.

Killing a tiny kid	*4,000 silver coins*
Killing a little girl	*8,000 silver coins*
Murdering a grown-up	*8,000 silver coins*
Boys, older girls and women	*24,000 silver coins*

You also had to pay the Wergild if you hurt someone. In fact, even if you just cut a child's hair off without permission you had to give their parents a load of money – a massive 1,800 silver coins! The Franks were very vain about their long hair!

So how did the Anglo Saxons (the name for all those tribes who'd settled in England) work out whether or not you were guilty?

They didn't. They let God decide.

Imagine you've been accused of something really bad like stealing a sackful of jewels. You deny it, but in order to find out if you're telling the truth, you have to undergo 'the ordeal by hot water'. Sounds fairly easy, doesn't it? Just sitting in a bath till your fingers go wrinkly. Well, no! It was slightly more unpleasant than that.

The Ordeal by Hot Water!

1 You spend three days praying and being kept without food.

2 Then, when you're practically starving, you're dragged to a church.

3 A severe-looking priest drops a ring into a cauldron full of boiling water . . .

4 . . . then you have to stick your arm in and grab the ring.

5 By now you're probably rolling around on the floor screaming in agony. If you're lucky your arm will be covered in blisters. If you're not, you won't have much skin left on it. Either way, your arm gets bandaged up. No Savlon, of course — no one's heard of germs.

6 Everyone waits three days, while you sit in a corner groaning.

7 Finally someone unwraps the bandages. If your arm's healed, it means God has decided that you were innocent and you're free to go and have a lie-down! If it hasn't healed, you are guilty and have to pay the fine. Although the good news is that you might not have to, because by now you've probably caught some horrible infection, so you'll most likely be a goner before they can get the money off you!

Luckily, young kids didn't often have to go through this. But whatever the king said went, and some kings could be a wee bit nasty. King Athelstan decided that anyone over the age of twelve who stole anything worth more than twelve pence should be executed. Later on, he had a change of heart. From now on all thieves under the age of fifteen would be allowed to live. That was the good news. The bad news was that if they fought back when they were arrested, or tried to escape, they'd be killed no matter how young they were.

Do you think all this sounds completely brutal?

Well, you ain't seen nothing yet!

OUCH, *THAT'S HOT!*

William the Conqueror invaded England in 1066, defeating the English King Harold, and William's French knights took over England and its law. After that, things got even more crazy.

Normans conquering!

From now on, if someone accused you of a serious crime you had to fight him, even if he was huge and muscly and you were a weed. Whoever won the fight was declared innocent; whoever lost was guilty. This might seem a bit unfair on the weed, but if you were a rich weed you could pay a professional fighter to take your place. So it was actually only hard on poor weeds.

Not only that, but if someone in your village killed a Norman, the whole village had to pay a crippling fine – even people who hadn't been there when the killing took place.

And there's more. The Normans also thought a good way to punish someone was to poke his eyes out and cut his willy off.

Pretty gruesome?

William's great-grandson King Henry II thought all this was pretty disgusting too. He decided he wanted to bring a bit of sense to the country's laws. From now on it wasn't going to be God who decided who was innocent or guilty by miraculously healing your blistery arm; judges and juries were going to run the show.

MORE NEW LAWS

OH GOODY!

Although Henry made a lot of changes,
don't think the law went soft!
Kids who committed crimes were still punished.

Bad Kid no. 3
Thomas of Hordlegh

In 1299, an eleven-year-old boy called Thomas of Hordlegh was put on trial for murdering a five-year-old girl. He was hungry so he'd gone into her house to steal some bread, and when she tried to stop him he grabbed an axe and killed her. He then hid her body – but he was caught anyway.

Even though Thomas was only ten when he killed her, the judges decided he had to be hanged. Why? Because he'd hidden the body, so he must have known he'd done something really wrong. And if he was old enough to know, he was old enough to die.

What do you think? If you'd been the judge, would you have topped Thomas?

The judge who sentenced Thomas to death was called Henry Spigurnel, and he wasn't always so harsh. A few years after Thomas met his horrible end, Spigurnel stood up in court and argued that everyone needed to go a bit easier on kids. He said children shouldn't be judged at all if they were under seven, and under-twelves should be punished only if they'd done something really dreadful.

This next bit is so disgusting it's probably best to read it with your eyes shut!

Even though being hanged must have been absolutely dreadful, there was an even worse punishment on offer if you were caught trying to kill a king.

OK, ready? Get out the sick bucket.

First you'd be hanged by the neck until you were choking and gasping for air.

Next the executioner would slice open your belly and drag your guts out and show them to you. (Although if I'd been the guilty man, I don't think I'd have looked.)

Then he'd cut your head off, chop you up, and stick the bits up on poles all around town.

The idea was to scare people so much they wouldn't even think of stepping out of line in future. It'd work for me, that's for sure.

YUK! THAT'S DISGUSTING

Head here

Arm here

Arm here

Throw here

Not many people went to jail. Prisons were mostly places to keep someone for a few days before their trial. Think about it: you're the town mayor – why hide your criminals away in a dungeon when, for a fraction of the cost, you could haul them into the main square and cut off their hands, or stick them in the stocks for people to throw rotten veg at? You wouldn't even have to pay for the veg as the audience would bring their own!

In London there was one kind of prison that was reserved especially for kids. A lot of boys were sent away by their parents to learn a trade. They were called apprentices, and they had a terrible reputation for being troublemakers. If you were an apprentice who did something seriously wrong, the Chamberlain of London would order you to be put in a cell at a place called the Little Ease, which was so tiny you couldn't stand up or lie down. You'd be left there until your cramp was such agony that you'd never be bad again.

Medieval prisons could be a tight squeeze!

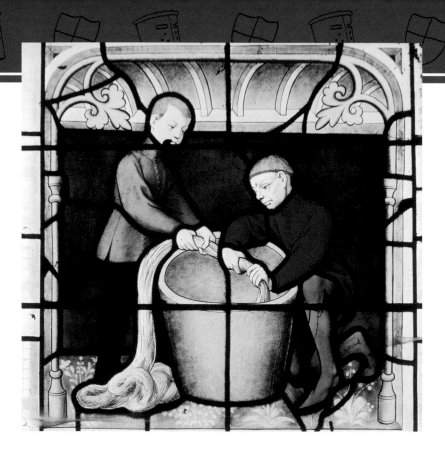

Sometimes apprentices got into trouble just for being a bit mouthy. In 1523 two teenagers called William Raynold and Thomas Appleford became bored with their job working for a cloth dealer. They started doing impressions of him and his wife, taking the mickey to make each other laugh. They were so good at it that they began performing for their mates, and were soon doing stand-up comedy routines for the regulars in the local pub.

But their boss found out, and he wasn't amused. Their punishment? He cut handfuls of willow branches from a tree, stripped off the leaves and bark till they were whippy and sharp, then beat William and Thomas black and blue. Mind you, I'd probably do the same if I could get my hands on some of the rubbish comedians on the telly today!

Say No to Swords

But compared to the things lots of other apprentices were getting up to, this was tame stuff. If you think gangs of hoodies can be scary now, be grateful you didn't live in medieval London. The boys who Londoners were afraid of back then were law students – just the people you'd expect to be swotty goody-goodies. One summer evening in 1326 two gangs of them had a huge street fight. Things went from bad to worse, swords were drawn, and an innocent passer-by was killed.

That was just the start. There had been a big rebellion in the news, and another crowd of about 300 boys decided to do a full-on battle re-enactment. They split into two gangs; one side pretended to be the rebel army, the other became the queen's army. They headed off to the fields outside London for a nice day out, but before long the fun turned to carnage. Anyone who wasn't badly injured in the battle was taken away and locked in those tiny prison cells. No chance of community service for these lads.

Not all badly behaved apprentices were thrown into jail, of course.

Suppose you'd stepped out of line, but hadn't been quite as bad as your mates who'd been hacking away at other boys with their swords. There were plenty of other annoying punishments around. Unlucky John Everard was working as an apprentice for his uncle Alan in London in 1394, when they got into an argument. Of course, young John got the blame. His punishment was to give his uncle money to buy a new horse, then to bend down and help him climb on to it every time Alan wanted to go anywhere. A bit like being made to give your teacher some dosh to buy a car, and then having to clean the windscreen with your tongue every morning.

Best Days of Your Life?

Some boys were sent away to school rather than being made to learn a trade. Generally schoolboys weren't quite as wild as apprentices. Maybe that's because they were too scared or too badly injured to run around. At Westminster School in the 1200s, schoolboys were beaten for any of the following things:

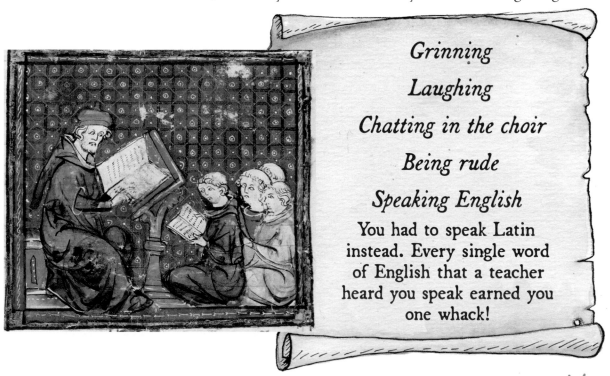

Grinning

Laughing

Chatting in the choir

Being rude

Speaking English
You had to speak Latin instead. Every single word of English that a teacher heard you speak earned you one whack!

A teaching assistant called an 'usher' sat on a special seat at the back of a medieval classroom. Ushers could be real sadists. They beat the living daylights out of you if you were late for school. They were even more unpopular than the teachers. Medieval school kids used to sing a song about how they dreamed of bumping into their usher at a stonemason's workshop or under a crab-apple tree – so they could get hold of a load of sharp stones or rotten apples to chuck at him.

Schoolboys would never have dreamed of complaining to their parents about the bruises they got at school. If they had, their mum and dad wouldn't have said, 'There, there, my darling, never mind; have a cuddle and a chocolate biscuit!' Instead they'd have been told to stop whingeing and given another good beating.

You Can't Beat a Beating

Why were people so violent in those days? After all, many modern parents believe that smacking their children would hurt them, or turn them into little thugs. But medieval mums and dads thought thumping their little darlings would teach them to be good. They believed this was really important because their kids would go to hell if they were naughty. There was a story about a mother whose daughter didn't do as she was told. Her mum wished out loud that the devil would take her – and a little red man with a pitchfork magically appeared and snatched the girl away.

'Whip your nippers from the age of three,
'til their twenty-fifth birthday!'
That was the advice of the time.

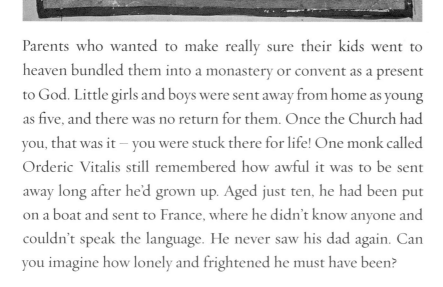

Parents who wanted to make really sure their kids went to heaven bundled them into a monastery or convent as a present to God. Little girls and boys were sent away from home as young as five, and there was no return for them. Once the Church had you, that was it – you were stuck there for life! One monk called Orderic Vitalis still remembered how awful it was to be sent away long after he'd grown up. Aged just ten, he had been put on a boat and sent to France, where he didn't know anyone and couldn't speak the language. He never saw his dad again. Can you imagine how lonely and frightened he must have been?

For a little kid learning to be a monk or a nun, life must have seemed like one long punishment. You had to eat all your meals standing up, and you were only allowed to play once a week.

The head of one monastery complained to a visitor that his boys didn't seem to mind being hit. 'Even though we don't stop beating them day and night', he said, 'they get worse and worse.'

I think I'd act up a bit too if I was a trainee monk and knew how miserable my life was going to be.

51

La outre voel paſſer
auoec ce notonier
ſi menrai auoec moi
mon neueu gadifier

But surely you wouldn't get whacked so much
if you were a spoilt little brat with a rich daddy,
would you?

Wrong!

If you were a rich kid, your parents and teachers thumped you
non-stop even if you were the son or daughter of a lord. And if
you were related to royalty, you were in big trouble. You might
just as well have walked around with an archery target drawn
on your back and a big sign saying 'Aim here, please!' – because
someone would always be out to get you.

Bad Kid no. 4
Ninja Revenge

The sons of Japanese noblemen had a lot of responsibilities. For instance, if their dad got killed, it was their duty to seek revenge. One thirteen-year-old Japanese boy called Kumawaka became a ninja legend this way. How cool is that?

Kumawaka's dad, Lord Suketomo, was arrested for rebelling against the king and was taken off by a troop of soldiers. Kumawaka followed them for many hours until they came to a big house with hundreds of rooms. He hung around, and eventually found out that his dad had been locked up in one of the rooms and was about to be executed. Kumawaka asked to see him, but the monk who was looking after his father said he couldn't. Kumawaka waited and waited, and was finally shown his dead dad's bones.

He was bitterly angry, and made a plan to get even. He pretended to be ill. I know this was a pretty unoriginal plan – thousands of kids do exactly the same thing to get off school – but Kumawaka had more sinister reasons. He was given a bed, and every day he lay in it, groaning and complaining about his stomach ache. But every night he'd get up and wander round the huge house, looking for the monk.

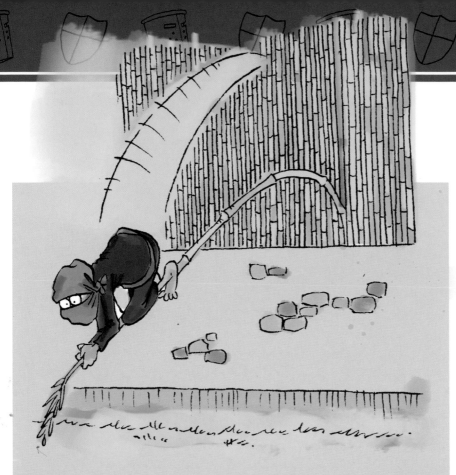

Finally he found him, snoring away in his bedroom. There was a light on, and Kumawaka didn't want to make a noise and wake the monk up, so instead he opened a window and let an enormous swarm of moths fly in. They fluttered their wings round the candles so furiously that they blew the flames out and the room was plunged into darkness. Then Kumawaka tiptoed round the room till he found the monk's sword, killed the monk and ran off. The guards rushed into the room, saw Kumawaka's bloody footprints, chased after him and cornered him. Kumawaka was stuck – the house was surrounded by thick bamboo, a moat and a high wall. But like a proper ninja, he climbed up a bamboo branch right to the tip, until it bent all the way down to the other side of the wall. Then he made his escape.

Live Posh, Die Young

Probably the most famous royal crime victims in British history are the 'Princes in the Tower'. Edward was twelve and Richard was ten in 1483 when their dad, King Edward IV, died and Young Edward was made King. Their uncle Richard, Duke of Gloucester, promised to look after both boys until they grew up. He put them both in a very safe place. Wasn't that kind of him? Not really – the safe place was the Tower of London, a damp, cold prison full of beetles and spiders.

Then Richard made himself king, and guess what? The boys disappeared and were never seen again. Who could have bumped them off? Over 500 years later we're still not sure what happened, but I bet you're thinking what I'm thinking!

Nottingham Castle

Another English royal, King John, the baddie in the Robin Hood stories, also saw the plus points of getting rid of a young relative. The story goes that John got drunk one night and murdered his sixteen-year-old nephew with his own hands, then chucked him in a river with a stone tied to him.

But one teenager wasn't enough for King John. A few years later he got rid of a whole classroom's worth at one go. He'd been fighting some pesky Welsh chieftains, and had taken twenty-eight of their sons hostage. He let them live in Nottingham Castle for a while, but got bored with them and hanged them in a row from the castle walls – nice bloke!

Yes, whether it was hitting kids, executing them, or sending a six-year-old girl off to be a nun for the rest of her life, medieval people would have disagreed with us about the best way to bring up children. But I'm sure they thought they were right, just as your parents do today!

What Happened When

450   *The Jutes, Saxons and Angles start turning up in Britain.*

476   *Invading hairy blokes with swords smash the mighty Roman Empire.*

793   *Viking raiders start attacking Britain.*

1066   *William the Conqueror turns up in England and — guess what? — conquers it. And he's brought some crazy new laws with him.*

1078   *Building work begins on the Tower of London, where for hundreds of years prisoners will have a rotten time.*

1085   *Ten-year-old Orderic Vitalis gets sent to France for a fun-free life as a monk.*

1095   *The Pope orders the First Crusade against the Muslims in the Holy Land.*

1203   *King John tops his nephew Arthur.*

1206–1227   *Genghis Khan starts the mighty Mongol Empire, by chopping people up all the way from China to Europe.*

1215   *The Church puts a stop to trial by ordeal. From now on, a fair trial means a judge and jury instead of blisters and bandages.*

1326   *Gang fight! London apprentices meet up for a big punch-up with added swords.*

1347–1352   *The gruesome disease they call the Black Death sweeps through Europe, killing people quickly and disgustingly.*

1483   *Princes Edward and Richard head off to the Tower of London, never to be seen again!*

1492   *Christopher Columbus leaves Spain to sail to Asia, but bumps into America instead.*

Chapter 3

Witches, morris dancing and hangings

Which explains why a strange thing ran up William Somers's leg

For a thousand years most people in western Europe had been Christians who followed the Pope in Rome and did whatever he said. But in the 1500s, round about four hundred years after William the Conqueror had invaded England, a bunch of rebels decided they weren't happy with the Pope and his Catholic religion. They started protesting, and came up with a new kind of Christianity; they called themselves Protestants.

From then on you didn't just have to go to church, you had to choose which sort, Catholic or Protestant. And what sort of Protestant? Soon there were plenty. There were Lutherans, Calvinists…not to mention Baptists, True Baptists, Anabaptists and Blue-kneed Baptists (actually I made the last one up but you get my point!). And whichever one you chose, it was bound to get up someone's nose and get you into trouble.

The safest thing was to believe in whatever religion the king believed in. Because if you didn't, you could end up being barbecued on a blazing fire in the middle of the town square.

But working out which religion the kings and queens of England supported wasn't easy because they kept changing the rules. Here's the religious news, blow by blow:

ROUND 1 – 1534

NO CATHOLICS!

HENRY VIII

King Henry VIII (the big bloke with six wives) loves the Pope. Then he decides he doesn't like him after all. He throws a tantrum and starts the Church of England. If you're a Catholic, you might as well jump straight on the bonfire.

Henry dies and his son **Edward VI** gets the crown. Edward is even more Protestant than his dad, so it's time for lots more Catholics to get sizzled!

ROUND 2 – 1547

DEFINITELY NO CATHOLICS!

EDWARD VI

ROUND 3 – 1553

NO PROTESTANTS!

MARY I

Edward dies young and his sister **Mary** is made queen. She's a Catholic through and through. She says everyone who turned Protestant was wrong. Time for the Catholics to jump out of the fire; it's the Protestants' turn to jump on and cover themselves with barbecue sauce.

After just five years, **Elizabeth I** gets to be queen. She's much more even-handed. What a relief! Everyone nervously begins to wash the sauce off their burning bottoms.

Not everyone was off the hook, though. People who believed in the 'wrong' things could still be given some terrible punishments. Even kids sometimes got into serious trouble for having the wrong faith.

Some children who lived in Bristol had parents who'd picked a very dangerous religion. Nowadays Quakers are famous for making porridge and being peaceful, but in the 1680s they were thought of as troublesome rebels.

THEY DON'T *LOOK* LIKE TROUBLE-MAKERS!

All the grown-up Quakers in Bristol were thrown in prison, but their kids weren't put off: they carried on having Quaker meetings of their own. For a couple of months the local constable tried to get them to stop. He put the children in the stocks, and beat them up again and again, but they kept on having meetings. Eventually he was so angry he sent them to prison. Kids like eleven-year-old Patience Herne and her seven-year-old sister Mary were kept in stinking, overcrowded cells, and stayed there for about five years until at last, in 1687, the new king, James II, announced that people should be free to worship God however they liked — and finally the Bristol Quakers were let out.

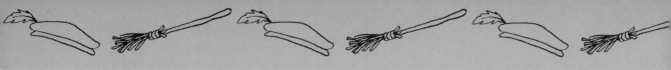

Are You a Good Kid?

If grown-ups tell you to 'be good', what exactly do they mean? Do they want you to stop fighting? Share things? Or just shut up so they can read the paper? Perhaps it would help if they sorted out what they meant before they had a go at you! In the 1500s a very clever Dutch man called Erasmus wrote down a list of ten things good children should never do. How many 'nevers' do you score?

1 *I never have a dirty nose with snot dangling from it.*

2 *I never bite people.*

3 *I never lick my lips like an animal.*

4 *I never cough in someone's face.*

5 *I never yawn when someone's speaking.*

6 *I never laugh like a maniac.*

7 *I never have a stupid fit of the giggles.*

8 *I never spit at people . . .*

9 *. . . or gob on the ground and walk away.*

10 *I never slouch, shuffle, lean, or generally look like a slob.*

If you got 10 'nevers' – you're a big liar and should be sent to bed without any supper.

If you got 9 – you think you're so great, don't you? But I bet you've got a few disgusting habits you don't tell anyone about.

If you got between 5 and 8 – go and live in the farmyard with the rest of the pigs.

Between 1 and 4 – you make me want to puke.

If you got 0 – yeah, that's what I got too.

The trouble with a lot of Protestants was that they didn't just dislike the bad things the Catholic Church had got up to (like making shedloads of money from the poor, and keeping it to themselves). They also wanted to ban the fun things!

Carol singing isn't wicked, is it? It's just a bunch of tone-deaf people dressed in scarves and bobble hats going round jangling a tin. But Henry VIII hated it. In his time children used to go from house to house, singing, dancing and collecting money, not just at Christmas, but on holy days all through November and December . . . and for a laugh they dressed up as priests, bishops or pantomime dames. But the king decided this was too Catholic – just the sort of thing God didn't want people to get up to. So he made a Royal Proclamation telling them to stop it RIGHT NOW. And to take off those silly priest costumes while they were at it, because they looked ridiculous . . . and a bit Catholic!

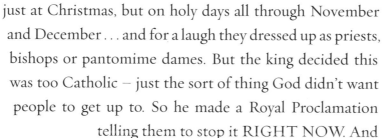

There were plenty of other things God didn't approve of, apparently. Priests could punish you for doing any of these terrible things:

- not going to church

- dancing on a Sunday

- refusing to say the Ten Commandments

- morris dancing (Mind you, I'm with them on that one!)

A lot of people were even more strait-laced than King Henry. They were called **Puritans** and they thought other Protestants weren't nearly Protestant enough. Puritans were famous for wearing strange black-and-white clothes and not having fun.

It wasn't much of a laugh being a kid with Puritan parents. You were supposed to be as godly and miserable as the grown-ups. You were beaten for all kinds of things, like laughing on a Sunday, or running, whistling or humming on any day of the week.

Basically, anyone who was a bit cheerful must have been in constant trouble. But you probably weren't cheerful very often – Puritan children weren't even allowed to celebrate their birthdays.

How to Punish a Prince

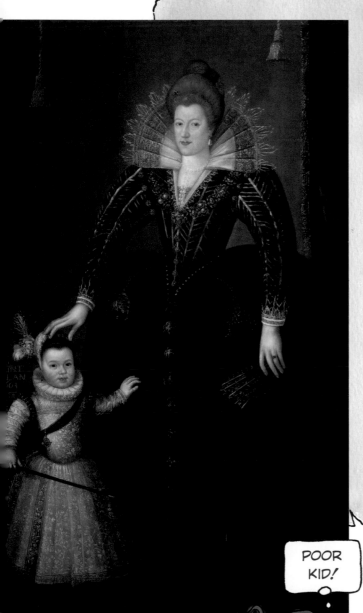

King Henri IV of France's son Louis was beaten every day first thing in the morning, starting when he was just two years old. He'd often wake up screaming in the night because he was so scared of what was in store for him. His dad died when Louis was eight, at which point you might have thought the beatings would stop. But the king had already written to Louis's teacher telling her to keep hitting him, which she did! Poor little Louis was even whipped on the morning he became the new king. He never forgot this awful treatment. Even when he was a grown-up, he still had nightmares about the thrashings he'd been given when he was a kid.

POOR KID!

Pilgrims meeting the neighbours

Some Puritans were so unhappy with the Church in England that in the 1630s they began leaving for **America**, where they could be as religious as they liked without other people telling them to get a life.

One of the worst things an American Puritan kid could be accused of was swearing at his parents. Obviously that's a pretty disrespectful thing to do, but personally I don't think you should be executed for it. Nevertheless, that's what the American Puritans decided was a fair punishment.

Some children managed to escape the death sentence though. In 1679 a boy named **Edward Bumpus** (yes, that really was his name, I'm not making it up!) got angry with his parents, swore at them and hit them. Seems that Edward was for the big chop, big time! But no – the lucky boy was found to be 'crazy-brained', so instead of being killed, he was just tied to a post and whipped.

Spot the Witch

The most terrible thing a child could do in those days was to call someone a witch. Back then being a witch didn't just mean dressing up in a pointy hat and waving a few plastic spiders about. In the 1600s people were really scared of witches. Almost everyone believed that a witch could curse you and even kill you with magic. They also thought that if you caught one, you should tie her to a stake and burn her to death!

In the little American town of Salem in the 1690s, three girls named **Ann Putnam** (aged twelve), **Abigail Williams** (aged eleven) and **Elizabeth Parris** (aged nine) started having fits, screaming gibberish and accusing their neighbours of witchcraft. They looked so weird and scary that everyone thought they must have had an evil spell cast on them! The vicar demanded to know who'd done it, and the answer was terrifying. There wasn't just one witch at work, there was a whole group of them! The girls named several people, and those people named even more people – and soon nineteen men and women had been hanged for witchcraft. All sorts of people were named as witches, even a four-year-old girl.

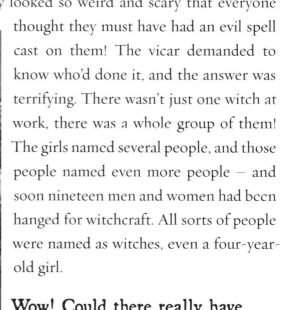

Wow! Could there really have been so many witches in a little town like Salem?

Actually, no! Four years later Ann fessed up: the whole thing had been make-believe. What a horrid girl!

You'd think someone might have guessed, because the first people the girls had named as witches were all people they didn't like much in the first place. That's one dreadful way to get your own back on your enemies.

The same sort of thing happened in England. There was a preacher in Leicestershire who was famous for getting rid of demons. One night he went to a tavern where a few locals were listening to a young pub singer called **William Somers.**

The preacher pointed an accusing finger at William and said there were devils inside him. Sure enough, the boy immediately started speaking gobbledegook, and a weird voice came out of him even though his mouth was closed.

You can imagine how quickly word got round. Soon William was a local celeb. People said his belly swelled up before their very eyes, and a strange *thing* ran up his leg and into his mouth, although no one was quite sure what it was. Creepy or what?

Then, just like the girls from Salem, William started spotting witches. He told the preacher who they were, and the preacher got thirteen people arrested.

In the end, William was found out and got arrested himself. The naughty little chappie admitted that the preacher had taught him to act weirdly. He'd even given William a special powder to make him foam at the mouth. The preacher was sent to prison, and the innocent 'witches' managed to escape being toasted.

Eventually the whole notion of witchcraft died out, thank goodness, but not before tens of thousands of people had been burned, hanged, drowned or tortured.

Little Beggars

Meanwhile some serious changes had been happening in Britain. The population had shot up, towns were getting really crowded, and there were lots more poor people. Many of them wandered all over the country looking for money or a job, but all these homeless people made the rich very scared. They thought if someone didn't have a home or a job, they were bound to be up to no good. They brought in new laws that said you could be punished for being a vagrant or a vagabond – in other words, for being homeless with no work.

And these laws applied not only to adults, but to children too. If anyone between five and fourteen years old was caught begging in the streets, they could be seized, and given away to a craftsman as an apprentice. That meant that for years they'd have to work for nothing, and when they were a bit older, if they tried to run away they'd get into even worse trouble. Children over twelve who attempted to escape could be whipped in public.

But even though the laws were so strict, lots of country children moved to the cities because they couldn't find work or food in the countryside. Just imagine how scary it must have been to walk around a big town at night when there were no electric street lights.

Spot the pickpocket!

There were no police either, and that meant there were plenty of dishonest opportunities for hungry young girls and boys. Nicking things was the quickest way to make money, and there wasn't too much risk of getting caught.

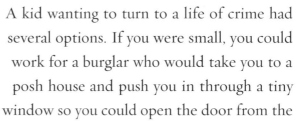

A kid wanting to turn to a life of crime had several options. If you were small, you could work for a burglar who would take you to a posh house and push you in through a tiny window so you could open the door from the inside and let him in. But you had to be light on your feet – knocking over the candlesticks could wake everyone up.

Or you could go to a special school for pickpockets run by criminals, where you had to pass a test a bit like those steady-hand games with buzzers. You had to reach into pockets which were dangling from the ceiling by bits of string, without setting off the alarm bells that were fixed to them.

Even if you had an honest job, you could earn a bit of cash on the side by helping a gang. 'Link-boys' used to carry torches through the streets at night to show people the way home. But dishonest ones sometimes led a rich person down a dark alley where a gang of thieves was waiting to mug him, and the link-boy would get a share of the cash.

It might have been easy money, but if you were caught the consequences could be terrifying. The worst punishment was the death penalty. As the crime rate rose, more and more crimes could get you killed. **By 1750 you could be hanged for:**

FORGING MONEY . . .

STEALING ANYTHING WORTH MORE THAN A SHILLING . . .

IMPERSONATING AN EGYPTIAN (NO – THIS DOESN'T MEAN WALKING SIDEWAYS WITH LOTS OF EYELINER ON – IT MEANS PRETENDING TO BE A GYPSY FORTUNE-TELLER) . . .

BURNING A PILE OF STRAW . . .

KILLING A RABBIT THAT WASN'T ON YOUR LAND . . .

GOING OUT WITH YOUR FACE COVERED WITH SOOT (SO PEOPLE COULDN'T IDENTIFY YOU IF YOU DID SOMETHING WRONG).

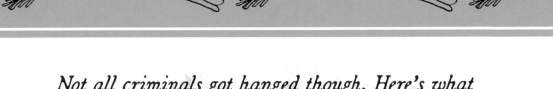

Not all criminals got hanged though. Here's what happened to a few kids from London in the 1690s who got caught and taken to court.

Name: Lawrence Noney **Description:** 'A black boy'
Crime: Theft. Stole a stick with a silver point on the end, worth four pounds and fifteen shillings. They knew he'd done it, because they found the head in his pocket. But luckily the head was the expensive bit, so once he'd given it back the court decided he'd only stolen a stick. That meant he couldn't be hanged, because the stick wasn't valuable enough.
Sentence: 'Lucky' Lawrence got a whipping instead, all through the streets of London. The jammy beggar!

Name: Mary Middleton **Age:** 7 or 8
Crime: Theft. Stole several items from a solicitor named Thomas Nichols, including two silver spoons and a scarf.
Sentence: Had the letter 'T' for 'thief' burned into her thumb with red-hot metal. Pretty horrible, but better than being hanged!

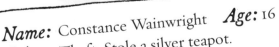

Name: Constance Wainwright **Age:** 16
Crime: Theft. Stole a silver teapot.
Sentence: Death, but she got let off and put in prison instead. Lucky girl? Not really. She set fire to the prison and was hanged for that.

Bored with Beatings?

Parents in Europe beat their kids with sticks so often it probably gave them arm-ache, and it must have worn out a lot of sticks. For a change, they could have tried some of these exotic foreign punishments, which were all the rage with the Aztec Indians in Mexico:

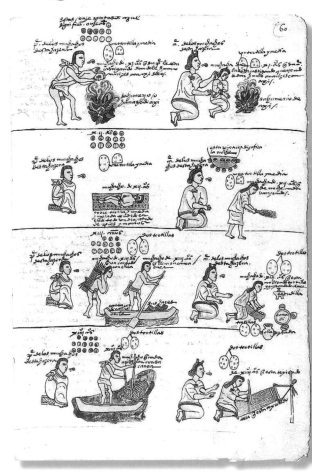

Being held over burning red chilli peppers so your eyes stung

Being made to work at night in the dark

Being tied up and stuck in a muddy hole

Being stung with a prickly leaf

What Happened When

1517 A German monk called Martin Luther starts protesting about the Church. It catches on, and soon there are Protestants all over the place.

1530 Erasmus writes a list of things that good kids don't do.

1534 Henry VIII makes himself supreme head of the Church of England, elbowing out the Pope completely.

1536 Harsh new laws against begging mean that kids on the street can be put to work, and whipped if they run away.

1541 Henry VIII makes a Royal Proclamation to stop the terrible sin of house-to-house carol singing.

1547 Edward VI turns England even more Protestant.

1553 Mary I turns England Catholic.

1558 Elizabeth I turns England Protestant again (by now everyone is really dizzy!).

1610 Prince Louis of France becomes king — but he still gets smacked every day!

1620 Puritans start heading to America to be properly religious, and stop their kids having birthday parties.

1642–1649 England is torn apart by civil war, and King Charles I loses his head.

1666 The Great Fire of London stops the plague — so it's not all bad.

1682 Quaker kids in Bristol get put in the stocks, whipped, and thrown in jail for their religion.

1692 Three girls in Salem, America, start calling people some very dangerous names — like 'witch'!

Chapter 4

Policemen, hooligans and transportation

Which offers you a free trip to Australia . . . in chains!

Imagine you are sitting on one of those long plastic seats in your local shopping centre talking to your mate Chesney on your mobile, when suddenly two burly blokes rush into the coffee shop opposite, mug a woman behind the counter, grab the notes out of her till and run back out again.

What's the first thing you'd do?

Hide?

Maybe – but they'd spot you straight away if you tried to hide under one of those long plastic seats.

How about saying, 'Hey, Chezzer, I've just seen a terrible crime. Let's get a gang of our friends together and a small dog, and search for clues.'?

No, that would be pathetic. That's just what kids do in stupid books. If you had any sense at all you'd probably yell, 'Get off the line, Chezz! I've got to phone 999!' And with a bit of luck the coppers would arrive shortly afterwards, and thanks to your prompt phone call they'd nab the criminals, and you'd get a small reward and your picture in the paper.

But 250 years ago, life wasn't like that, partly because the mobile phone hadn't been invented yet, but more importantly because neither had the police! There were people called thief-takers, who got paid by rich victims of crime to catch the bloke who'd stolen their jewels, but there weren't any cops in uniform whose job was to keep the streets safe.

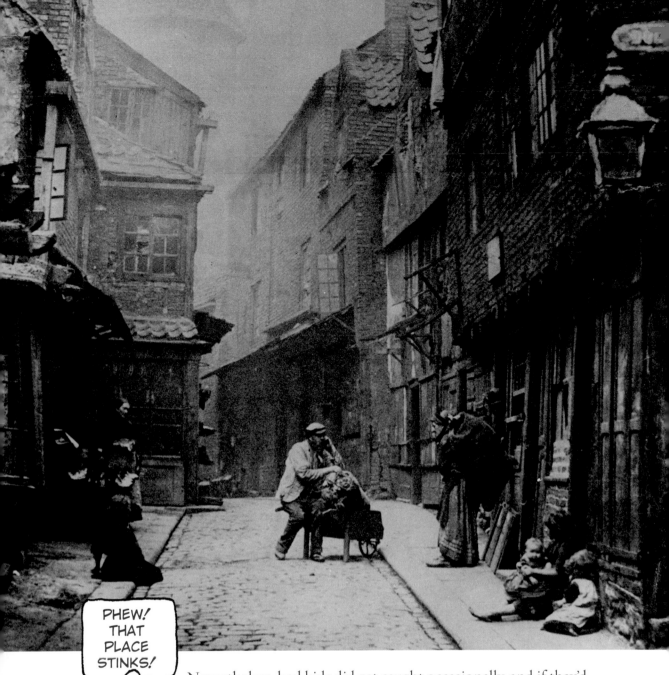

PHEW! THAT PLACE STINKS!

Nevertheless, bad kids did get caught occasionally, and if they'd committed a terrible crime they were hanged or flogged or suffered some other foul and disgusting punishment. But if they'd done a not-too-terrible crime, no one was really bothered about them, and with a bit of luck they got away with a smack on the bottom or a whack round the ear.

Around the year 1750 big factories started being built in cities all over Britain, and a whole army of workers was needed to operate them. More poor people poured in from the countryside than ever before, and the towns got bigger and bigger. Soon there were millions of dark streets, thousands of unlocked doors, and hundreds of bad kids on the lookout for stuff to nick.

A new system was needed to make sure everyone behaved themselves, *especially* those pesky kids.

All around the country, little bands of crime-solvers called policemen were set up, with special uniforms so people could recognize them. They were known as 'Peelers' or 'Bobbies' because the politician who was in charge at the time was called Robert Peel. They wore long blue coats and specially reinforced top hats, which made them look taller and also protected them from doinks on the head. The only weapon they carried was a wooden truncheon. Their job wasn't just to catch people who'd committed a crime – they were also supposed to walk around the streets on patrol, looking big and important and scaring the bejeezus out of everyone to stop them even thinking about doing anything wrong.

Robert Peel

GIVE US A SMILE, MATE!

Bristol City police practising their cutlass drill

You might have expected them to catch loads of fierce, scary crooks, but in fact the easiest people to arrest were kids. Peelers were allowed to pull children in for the silliest little crimes like . . .

kicking a ball near a sign that said 'No Ball Games'

begging

hanging around outdoors between sunset and eight in the morning without a good excuse

selling matches in the street

flying kites flying kites!!
(I've written this one twice just in case you didn't believe me the first time.)

Though it might be hard to believe, children were even sent to prison for daft little 'crimes' like these.

But though this seems bad enough, what do you think happened to you if a policeman caught you doing something really serious?

Well, if you were really unlucky . . . transportation!

Aaaaaaaaaaaaaaaaarrrrrrrrgggggghh!!

Pardon!

'Transportation' was the word for sending someone away to a foreign country, forcing them to do a horrible job, and not letting them come back to Britain again for ages, if at all. It must have seemed a pretty clever wheeze at the time. After all, it wasn't as upsetting as hanging people in the town square, and it was less hassle than keeping them in prison for the rest of their lives. And there wasn't much chance they'd escape and come home and commit another crime, because they'd gone so far away they'd never be able to find their way back.

In the late 1700s, Britain started transporting criminals to **Australia**, twelve thousand miles away.

They were packed into ships, stuffed below decks like seasick sardines, and chained together with rats and cockroaches crawling all over them.

Some of the prisoners were so young they shouldn't have been allowed to go into town on their own, let alone sail halfway

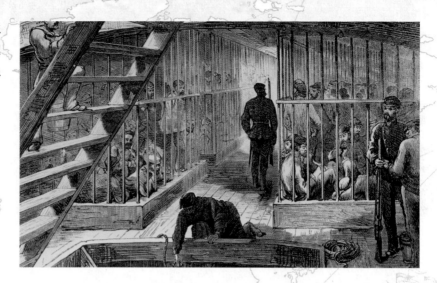

Prisoners aboard a transport ship bound for Australia

round the world. James Grace, aged eleven, was on the very first prison ship out to Australia. His crime was that he'd stolen ten yards of ribbon and a pair of silk stockings. Elizabeth Hayward, thirteen, was on board too; she'd nicked a linen gown and a silk bonnet. The youngest passenger was nine-year-old John Hudson, who'd been a chimney sweep back home in England, but had stolen some clothes and a pistol. I can't imagine he'd have been much use once he got to Australia — hardly any houses out there had proper chimneys!

Convicts going to the waterside at Blackfriars for transport to Australia

The journey lasted eight months, and a lot of prisoners died before they got there. But if the voyage was dangerous, it was even more dangerous when they arrived. There wasn't enough food, everyone kept getting ill, and there were loads of poisonous spiders and snakes. It's amazing that anyone survived at all.

Kid Prison

Not all naughty kids ended up in Australia. Back home, more and more young criminals were being sent to prison, although this created more problems than it solved. All kinds of prisoners got banged up together – grown-ups and kids, axe-murderers and kite-flyers. So the kids who got sent there didn't become better behaved – instead they learned how to be better criminals, because the grown-up prisoners they mixed with taught them the best ways to rob, mug and pick pockets.

Eventually the government realized that kids needed prisons of their own, and they began to be separated from adult criminals.

Not that their prisons were any nicer than the ones the grown-ups were sent to.

The British navy had a spare ship that was pretty smashed up from being in so many

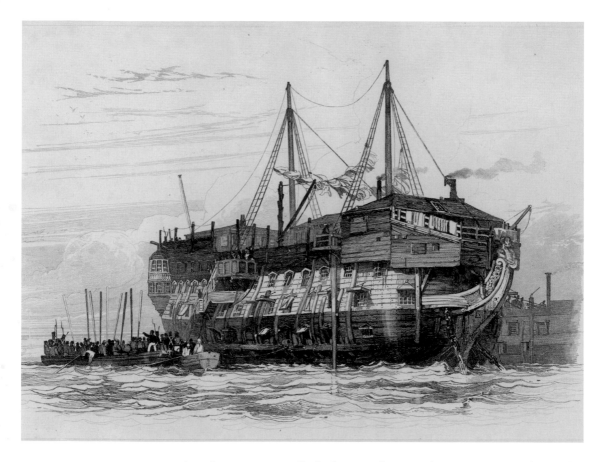

battles. It was called the *Euralyus*, and it was moored on the River Thames at Chatham. It couldn't go anywhere because its masts had been shot off, so it was the perfect place to put bad kids – nasty, uncomfortable and, best of all, cheap.

Boys as young as nine were locked up in this hulk, with iron cuffs round their legs to stop them diving overboard.

Life there was incredibly boring. Turn the page to see what you had to do every single day.

Life on the Incredible Hulk

Oh yes, and if you stepped out of line, you got a taste of the **cat-o'-nine-tails.** This didn't mean eating a mutant moggy; the 'cat' was a special kind of whip, with nine ropes dangling from the handle to make each blow hurt nine times as much.

But that wasn't the scariest thing. The bullying was far worse. The older boys would beat you up and nick your food, which was a terrible thing to do to kids who were half-starved already. The violence was so bad that some boys used to break their own arms so they'd be sent to the sickbay for a while, where the bullies couldn't get them.

For fifteen years kids were sentenced to live on that hideous ship, until finally a new children's prison was set up on dry land. It was in the middle of nowhere, on the Isle of Wight, and it was called Parkhurst. The idea behind it was that boys who were going to be transported would be sent to Parkhurst first, where they'd learn to do farm work so they could get a job once they were in Australia. But Parkhurst was no swanky hotel. It was so nasty that after prisoners had spent a little while there, they couldn't *wait* to be sent to the other side of the world!

Parkhurst Prison

How to Make Nasty Kids Nice

By the 1900s grown-ups weren't satisfied with just locking up bad kids or sending them far away. They wanted to cure them of being criminals. They tried all kinds of things to turn these naughty little devils into sweet little angels.

Horrible Boys' Stuff

Some bad boys were offered the chance of a life of adventure on the high seas, serving in the Royal Navy. It was much more fun than being cooped up in a hulk, but they might end up fighting in a war and getting their arms and legs blown off.

Hold on tight! We don't want to become fish food

Horrible Girls' Stuff

Bad girls didn't go to sea, but they could be sent to a Magdalen Hospital instead. This meant learning the Bible, sewing and housework, so that when the time came to leave they could get a job as a servant, working seventeen-hour days, washing up and cleaning floors for the rest of their lives.

I'M OFF BEFORE THEY WASH ME!

If that kind of training didn't make them want to run away and turn to a life of crime, I don't know what would.

Horribly Unfair Stuff

There were also schools called industrial schools, where you got sent to learn farming (for boys) or housework (for girls). But you didn't have to have done anything wrong to end up in one. Children got sent to industrial schools just because someone thought they were *in danger* of becoming criminals! That included kids who hadn't committed a crime but were poor or homeless, or whose parents were criminals. How unfair!

So why were so many kids being punished? Were they really such a horrible lot? One certainly was. He lived in Kent, and his name, believe it or not, was **John Any Bird Bell**. If you had a daft name like that, I imagine you might be pretty angry. But however brassed off you were, there'd be no excuse for behaving like he did.

Bad Kid no. 5
John Any Bird Bell

John had a tough life. His dad, a farm worker, was out of work a lot, and his mum sold things from the back of a donkey cart. His family were so poor that he and his little brother James had to dig roots out of the ground to sell. He was already heading down the path to a life of crime by the time he was thirteen, stealing from local shops and houses. But then, in 1831, he went further – and became a murderer.

John's victim was a lad called Richard Taylor, who was the same age as John but quite a bit smaller. Richard was from a poor family too, and every week his dad sent him to a nearby town to pick up his benefit money. On the way, he'd often bump into John hanging around by the road. Normally Richard's little sister Mary Ann would go with him to get the money, but on Friday 4 March 1831, he went all by himself.

He picked up the cash in town, then set off home. He bumped into John and James Any Bird Bell, and John helpfully offered to show him a short cut through the woods to get back to his village. After they'd been walking for a while through the trees, John told Richard he was lost. Richard got scared and sat down to have a little cry, at which point John pounced on him, slit his throat with a knife and took his money.

Nearly ten weeks went by, and John carried on as though nothing had happened, even playing near the scene of the crime. Then one day a passer-by walking in the woods found Richard's body – and John was an obvious suspect, as he'd been seen with Richard on the day he went missing. He was arrested, and owned up to the murder. His trial was set for Friday 29 July.

The court was packed – funny how people get excited by gruesome murders, isn't it? The newspapers said that even though he'd committed a truly horrible crime he didn't look upset. But then I never trust what I read in the newspapers, do you? They also reckoned he was too short and ugly to be innocent, and had suspiciously cunning eyes.

The jury found John guilty, but they recommended that he shouldn't be executed because he was too young and he'd had a tough childhood. The judge disagreed – and sentenced John to death. On the Monday morning John was hanged in front of more than eight thousand people.

But that wasn't the end of the matter. His brother, James, got a job with a travelling show, going round fairs telling people the grisly details. He even used a wax model of the dead boy to illustrate exactly what had happened. There's nothing like a good live show, is there!

So Why Were Kids Executed?

A lot of grown-ups thought that if bad kids were able to get away with murder then other kids might go on killing sprees too, because they'd think they could get away with it. Hanging was supposed to put people off crime.

So when criminals were hanged, teachers took their pupils on trips to watch the execution, to teach them not to turn into murderers. This might be a fairly bloodthirsty way of learning, but at least it got you off a morning's school.

KEEP UP OR WE'LL MISS THE SHOW!

Celebrity Criminal
The Artful Dodger

By now even more gangs of pickpockets were appearing in London (like the ones we met in the last chapter). Charles Dickens made them famous in his book *Oliver Twist*, in which Oliver joins a gang led by the evil Fagin. The cheekiest and brightest of the pickpockets in the book is called the Artful Dodger, a character so brilliant and handsome that I myself was picked to play him on the West End stage when I was a kid.

There were other gangs of kids though who were far more terrifying than wussy me at the age of thirteen. In the 1890s people started panicking about violent posses of kids taking to the streets. On the August Bank Holiday of 1898 there was an explosion of fighting between rival gangs, and the newspapers picked up the story. A new kind of problem had been created, with a new name: **hooliganism!**

Me trying to look really artful and dodgery!

Hooligans hung around on street corners, swearing and spitting at people, robbing old ladies and attacking anyone who looked foreign. They even carried knives. One of their favourite hobbies was to walk along in big groups, blocking the pavement and beating up anyone who tried to get past them.

Hooligan Style

Fashion was as important in those days as it is now. Here's what you would have worn if you'd been a hooligan in the 1890s:

A DISTINCTIVE HAIRCUT: it was called the 'donkey fringe', short hair with long bits plastered down over your forehead.

A CAP: it was important to get this at just the right angle, pulled forward over your eyes so you couldn't be recognized easily, a bit like a hoody.

A LONG SCARF: it could get chilly on those street corners.

A BIG LEATHER BELT WITH A HEAVY METAL BUCKLE: it looked flashy, and you could take it off and use it as a weapon (until your trousers fell down).

BELL-BOTTOMED TROUSERS: tight at the knee and loose round the ankle.

A POSTCODE EMBLEM: just like today you needed something that'd show which gang you were in. For instance, in London, hooligans from Battersea wore velvet caps, and the gangs from Poplar wore tartan caps.

BIG BOOTS: ideal for kicking someone from another gang.

It seemed like bad kids were everywhere. People couldn't work out why. They came up with all kinds of reasons:

Children gamble too much, and when they run out of money they steal more.

Make them go to church! Otherwise, how will they know it's wrong to steal?

There aren't enough jobs! If kids can't work, they'll become nasty little pickpockets.

I blame the parents. If your mum and dad are thieves and drunkards, it's a pretty safe bet you'll turn out that way too.

I blame comics. They're full of gory stories about disgusting criminals like Dick Turpin the highwayman. They make crime ound glamorous and exciting; it's no wonder kids get excited by it.

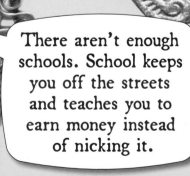

There aren't enough schools. School keeps you off the streets and teaches you to earn money instead of nicking it.

They should never have invented the bicycle. Now kids can move around really quickly, and can escape when you chase them.

Don't blame the cyclists! If the police lock up kids for stupid little things like throwing snowballs and whistling too loudly, the crime figures are bound to go through the roof! But it doesn't necessarily mean there are more bad kids.

OK, that's what the grown-ups thought. But why do you reckon so many kids seemed to be causing trouble?

And if you were a kid then, would you have been one of them?

What Happened When

1718 British judges start sending lots of criminals to America as a punishment, instead of hanging them. Sounds like a much better deal to me!

1756 The Maritime Society starts training bad boys to go into the navy.

1758 The first Magdalen Hospital for bad girls is set up.

1770 Captain Cook discovers Australia. Everyone's very surprised — including the people who already live there.

1771 The first cotton mill opens in England. Soon, factories will be everywhere.

1776 The Americans sign a Declaration of Independence, to say that Britain's not the boss of them any more. And we have to stop sending our prisoners there too.

1778 Britain starts transporting criminals to Australia instead.

1789 The French Revolution begins.

1825 Bad lads get locked up on the *Euralyus* hulk.

1829 The first 'Peelers' in the Metropolitan Police grab their truncheons and get ready for duty.

1837 Victoria becomes Queen of England.

1837 Charles Dickens writes about a gang of pickpocketing nippers in Oliver Twist.

1838 Parkhurst Boys' Prison opens.

1857 Industrial schools open across Britain.

1880 School becomes compulsory until you're ten. This is supposed to be a good thing, not just another kind of prison!

1886 The first bicycles in Britain go on sale. Now naughty rascals can pester grown-ups at a much higher speed.

1898 HOOLIGANS start putting the boot in.

Chapter 5

Hoodies, punks and ASBOs

What are Toddler Tongs?
Here's a clue . . .
they're tiny, Scottish and
very mean!

Once upon a time, there was a plucky general called Lord Baden-Powell, who was a famous war hero. During a long siege in South Africa in 1900 he was helped out by young boys known as 'scouts', who ran around doing odd jobs for him, like delivering messages to his men. Baden-Powell was really impressed by these boys, and he started thinking how great it would be if kids all over the world could learn to make themselves as useful as those lads.

Baden-Powell 1908

So a few years later he picked twenty British boys, some rich, some poor, and took them for a camping trip on Brownsea Island in Dorset, to see if his 'Scouting' experiment would work on them.

The boys spent a week learning how to survive outdoors, playing games like hunting each other, going out in boats spearing fake 'whales' (but with real harpoons!) and listening around the campfire to Baden-Powell's tales of bravery and adventure. He was so excited by the experience that the next year he published a book called *Scouting for Boys*, which was full of handy tips about how to track animals, keep your clothes dry when you're camping, and stop yourself from getting thirsty when you're out on a run (you chew a pebble, apparently – which seems not only daft but dangerous to me!).

Boys loved it, Scouting swept the nation, and thousands of kids got into the habit of doing 'good turns' – in other words doing

little jobs for free, like mowing someone's lawn or carrying an old person's shopping for them.

BUT I DIDN'T **WANT** TO CROSS THE ROAD!

But there were plenty of bad kids who thought the Scouts were nerds. Baden-Powell made the first Boy Scouts wear uniforms like his original scouts in Africa, with short trousers, big cowboy hats and green neck-scarves. They even carried broomsticks to use as hiking sticks. This may have been sensible clothing for the African bush, but some bad kids thought it looked peculiar, and used to throw spuds at the Scouts to try to knock their hats off.

Then in 1909 an American businessman came to London and got lost in the fog, and a little boy offered to show him the way back to his hotel. When they got there, the

businessman tried to give him some money as a thank-you. But the boy said no: he said he was a Scout and he was just doing his 'good turn'. The businessman was so impressed he went home and started the Boy Scouts of America. Soon there were Wolf Cubs for younger boys to go to, and Girl Guides and Brownies for their sisters. The organization got bigger and bigger. Boys and girls from all over the world would meet up and sing songs around the fire at enormous Scout camps. Wasn't that nice!

Hang on a minute, though! How come people were suddenly trying to make kids good by giving them free camping holidays and real harpoons?

What about hanging them and transporting them to Australia in chains for being bad? Had all that stopped?

Well, **yes**. A big new idea had come into fashion.

People had always thought that if you were a bad kid, you stayed a bad kid for the rest of your life, unless you were so frightened of being hanged that you mended your ways, or became religious and miraculously turned good.

But at the beginning of the twentieth century some grown-ups started thinking differently. Suppose bad kids were basically good, and only turned bad because they'd had an unhappy childhood, and had been beaten and abused and generally made to feel pretty awful?

If that was the case, you didn't need to punish bad kids — you could make them become good by *treating them right*.

So from now on fewer kids got banged up in prison. Instead they were sent to a juvenile court, with a magistrate in charge who was an expert on criminal kids. New children's lock-ups called **borstals** were built. They were supposed to be softer than prison, and teach kids to be good after they got out, but I don't think you or I would have fancied going to one!

The idea behind borstals was that a special school with a strict routine could cure you of your slouching, criminal, layabout ways. The guards were pretty fierce, shouted at you a lot and kept you busy gardening, painting, washing clothes, keeping pigs – and doing hours and hours of PE.

And there were no dozy mornings lying in. At 5.30 a.m. you had to wake up and head straight outdoors to do military drill, where you'd march around in neat lines, obeying every single order the instructor screamed in your face.

But at least borstals were better than prison, and some kids even liked the routine. Not that these new ideas stopped all children from being bad.

There were still plenty of gangs: the Peaky Blinders in Birmingham, the Redskins in Glasgow and the Bengal Tigers in Manchester. But the scariest were another Manchester gang who called themselves the Napoo. They were a bunch of right little stinkers, who wore pink hankies round their necks, and had cut-throat razors sticking out of their waistcoat pockets. But their weapons weren't just for fighting. They'd obviously been watching too many films about Red Indians scalping their victims, because they copied them by nicking people's hair. It was the fashion for young girls to wear long plaits, and the Napoo used to get on trams at night, sneak upstairs, sit behind the female passengers, slash off their plaits and run away – whooping like Indians who'd nabbed a scalp!

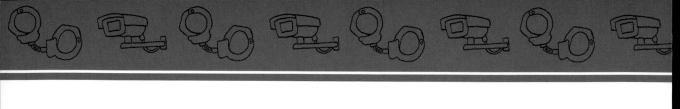

Busted!

In the 1930s, a bunch of kids got busted – not for being bad, but for trying to keep fit! Most people were pretty poor at that time, and lots of them took up hiking through the countryside as a hobby. But there weren't many footpaths, and walking over someone else's land was against the law. So when five hundred inner-city kids went for a walk in the Peak District in 1932, the coppers pounced, and five kids were sent to prison. (I don't think this would happen nowadays. Most people would be surprised and delighted if a bunch of British kids decided to go for a long ramble in the countryside!)

Weak Kids and Muscly Kids

Scientists tried hard to work out what caused kids to be bad in the first place. In 1949 an American expert on crime called William Sheldon came up with a weird new suggestion. He said that badness depended on the shape of kids' bodies. He said there were three types of boys:

ECTOMORPHS,
who were small, shy, weak and clever.

ENDOMORPHS,
who were friendly and slow-moving, with soft, round bodies.

MESOMORPHS,
who were muscly, aggressive and athletic.

Guess which ones he thought committed the most crimes? Yes, the muscly mesomorphs.

Maybe he was right, and all sporty boys should be locked up. On the other hand, maybe it was easier for them to commit crimes because they were fit, strong and agile, while the little nerds like me didn't bother because they knew they'd get caught.

But by the middle of the last century it seemed as though, apart from the street gangs, children might be turning good at last. There were Scout troops and lots of other clubs to get them doing good deeds, and borstals where the bad 'uns could get training and learn a new way of life. Maybe kids would soon stop being a nuisance altogether, there'd be no more trouble, and everyone would live happily ever after!

OR MAYBE NOT.

No one had counted on the new and terrifying monsters who were about to conquer the world . . .

TEENAGERS!!!

AARRGGHHH!

After the Second World War, something exciting began happening in America. It was big, it was rude, it was loud . . . it was rock 'n' roll. Soon kids all over the world were getting flashy haircuts and learning to play the electric guitar. A new name was invented for these crazy modern youngsters who spent all their time hanging out and dancing to the latest records. They were called

TEENAGERS!!!

And they got the blame for **everything**.

Rock 'n' roll drove normal kids wild. When the rock star Bill Haley's film *Rock Around the Clock* made it to Britain, teenagers found it so exciting they started riots in the cinemas, danced in the aisles and slashed the seats with razors. Suddenly there seemed to be a lot of aggravation around again. Half of all serious crimes were now being committed by kids under twenty-one.

But most teenagers just wanted a bit of fun. They'd got far more money than their parents had when they were young, because there were lots of well-paid jobs around. And like kids the world over, teenagers wanted to spend it on the latest music and the most fashionable clothes. They may have looked bad, weird and dangerous, but most of them were just trying to be trendy.

Teddy Boys

First appearance: 1950s

Distinguishing features: long jackets with velvet collars; hair in a quiff; drainpipe trousers; suede shoes

Type of badness: smashing up the cinema while watching the latest rock 'n' roll movie

Rockers

First appearance: late 1950s

Distinguishing features: leather jackets; greased hair; motorbikes

Type of badness: going to the seaside on bank holidays to fight mods

Mods

First appearance: late 1950s

Distinguishing features: neatly dressed, with sharp suits and haircuts; wear parka jackets in winter; ride around on Vespa scooters

Type of badness: going to the seaside on bank holidays to fight rockers

Hippies

First appearance: 1960s
Distinguishing features: tie-dye; beads and flowers in their hair; living on communes; nature, peace and love
Type of badness: smoking marijuana; forgetting to wash and falling asleep a lot

Skinheads

First appearance: late 1960s
Distinguishing features: very short hair; braces; big boots
Type of badness: starting fights at football matches

Punks

First appearance: mid-1970s

Distinguishing features: bin liners; safety pins through their ears; ripped clothes; hair dyed in mad colours

Type of badness: winding people up by spitting and swearing (although most of them were actually nice respectable teenagers just pretending to be horrid)

119

All around the world, gangs seemed to be becoming more and more scary. In America, street gangs were big news all through the 1980s. They sold drugs, had secret codes and symbols, and shot each other in full-on wars. Lots of kids were involved in them. One of the most notorious gangs in Los Angeles, the Crips, was started by a fifteen-year-old. Kids joined gangs to get money and respect, but found that if they tried to leave, the other gang members wouldn't let them.

By the 1990s, some grown-ups thought that all this being nice to bad kids and not hitting them had just turned them into spoilt brats. Wherever you looked, there were bad kids in the news.

Gang members in Los Angeles

Weird Words

Ever heard of a **tong**?

How about a **chib**?

Do you know what a **busy** is?

They're all words used by Glasgow gangs in the 1960s.

There had been a problem with gangs in Glasgow for over a hundred years. They fought over religion, over drugs, over territory, even over which gang should be in charge of the ice-cream vans!

Forty years ago there were lots of teenage gangs, and they were completely out of control. They had weird names like the Gorbals Cumbie and the Port Toi, but the scariest were the Tongs. They even had a junior version for younger thugs, called the Toddler Tongs, who were all aged between ten and thirteen. These gangs may have had daft names, but you'd be crazy to laugh at them because they often carried 'chibs' (weapons), usually knives or razors.

So you'd better hope the 'busies' were nearby. What were they? I'll give you a clue. If you were cornered by a 'tong' with a 'chib' and dialled 999, the 'busies' would probably come to your rescue.

In Liverpool in 1993 something really horrible happened. A two-year-old boy called James Bulger disappeared while he was out shopping with his mum. A couple of days later, he was found dead two miles away. After CCTV pictures were shown on the news, James's killers were caught – and shockingly they were two ten-year-old boys. No one could believe that kids could be that awful to each other. Newspapers said the boys were monsters and should be locked up in prison for the rest of their lives.

Pretty soon the news was full of young villains who'd not only committed loads of dreadful crimes, but weren't afraid of the police. Newspapers weren't allowed to print the names of kids who'd been arrested, so they gave them nicknames that made them sound like comic-book monsters . . .

Bad Kids 6, 7, 8 & 9
Rat, Balaclava, Boomerang and Spider Boy

There was **Rat Boy** (a fourteen-year-old who'd committed fifty-five offences and was found hiding in his estate's heating system) . . .

Balaclava Boy (who wore a mask) . . .

Boomerang Boy (who kept on coming back to court) . . .

. . . and **Spider Boy** (no, he didn't get bitten by a radioactive spider and develop superhuman strength; he had a mysterious talent for climbing high walls and sprinting over rooftops to get away from the police).

Stories like these made a lot of people very frightened of kids. They began to think that all children were bad kids, likely to smash up their schools, beat up old ladies, and destroy town centres. So adults have recently been trying some new ways to get kids to behave themselves.

*Here are a few of the new weapons
in the war on bad kids:*

ASBOs

If your local council or police force don't like the way you're behaving, they can get out an ASBO (or Anti-Social Behaviour Order) to stop you doing whatever you're up to.

This works because: it's much quicker and easier than taking you to court.

This doesn't work because: a lot of people think that ASBOs aren't fair, and some bad kids even feel quite proud when they're given one.

Bedtime — or Else

About twenty years ago some American cities banned all kids from going out at night.

This works because: the streets become much quieter.

This doesn't work because: it means kids aren't allowed to do ordinary, innocent things like visit their grandma, or go and buy some chips.

Ban Hoodies

Some shopping centres have outlawed kids from wearing hoodies.

This works because: some bad kids used to wear hoodies so their faces couldn't be seen on the CCTV cameras.

This doesn't work because: innocent kids' ears get cold.

Buzz Off

Until they're about twenty years old, kids can hear higher-pitched noises than adults can. A machine called the 'mosquito box' has recently been invented, which gives out an irritating whining noise that grown-ups can't hear. Some shopkeepers install them outside their shops to keep kids away.

This works because: bad kids don't go inside the shops to nick sweets and stuff.

This doesn't work because: good kids don't go inside the shops to buy sweets and stuff.

Anti-pop

Recently a number of shops and railway stations have been playing soft, gentle classical music through their loudspeakers to calm down bad kids.

This works because: lots of bad kids hate classical music and would rather go anywhere else than have to listen to it.

This doesn't work because: lots of kids don't even notice it's playing – and some rather like it!

Pretty Lighting

Some shopkeepers put pretty pink lights outside their shops. They think kids won't hang around because they'll look uncool if their faces have a pink glow.

This works because: it makes bad kids' spots show up.

This doesn't work because: pink can make you look quite attractive.

War Games

If you've ever run around the playground pointing your fingers at your mates and shouting, 'Bang bang, you're dead,' you might think it would be kind of fun to be a soldier. Take my advice: think again.

All around the world, there are thousands of children who are playing soldiers for real – and you don't want to run into them. In Uganda in Africa, there has been fighting going on since the 1980s. One of the groups doing the fighting is called the Lord's Resistance Army, and it's famous for being almost entirely made up of kids. These children attack defenceless villagers, cutting off people's lips, noses and ears and killing innocent people. Sometimes child soldiers will even kill their own families and friends to prove they're loyal to the army.

Why would anyone do those things, especially a kid?

Well, some kids join armies because there's an enemy they really want to fight. Some don't have any other way to get food. And many child soldiers are kidnapped and told they have to join the army, or else they'll be killed. The Lord's Resistance Army gives kids oil to rub on their skin. They tell them it's magic oil which will stop bullets so they needn't be frightened of being killed. They also tell them they'll be shot if they don't fight.

With everything you see on TV, you'd think it was kids' fault there are so many wars and that the planet's being destroyed!

So what about today's gangs?

Well, as you've seen, they're nothing new; there have been gangs of kids since ancient times. Most gangs are harmless – after all, a 'gang' can just mean a group of friends, and there's nothing wrong with hanging out with your mates, is there?

But some gangs are causing real problems. Younger and younger kids are getting involved in crime and, just like in the old days, once they've been in prison it's hard for them to get their lives back on track.

And what about the killings? Teenagers are being murdered by other teenagers, sometimes just for a pathetic excuse like 'they were looking at me the wrong way'.

As always, everyone's looking for a solution – but they haven't found one yet.

Grown-ups have tried **hitting** bad kids.

They've tried **not hitting** bad kids, and being nice to them instead.

They've tried throwing bad kids in **prison**.

They've tried sending bad kids to **special schools**.

They've even tried sending bad kids to **Australia**, hoping they never come back.

But after all the things grown-ups have tried in order to get bad kids to be good, they still don't seem to be winning. Kids keep on being naughty, and for all sorts of reasons: because they're hungry, because they want things that aren't theirs, because they're angry, because they want to impress their mates, or because they're scared of what will happen if they don't . . . And those reasons probably won't ever go away.

Who knows what those dastardly adults will try next? Maybe bad kids will be given really itchy diseases as a punishment, or have their skin dyed bright orange for a year so everyone can spot them. But one thing's for sure: grown-ups are not going to give up trying to make you be good!

What Happened When

1901   Queen Victoria dies and Edward VII becomes king.

1902   The first borstal opens in Kent, for boys aged sixteen to twenty-one.

1907   Robert Baden-Powell takes twenty lads to Brownsea Island for a new kind of camping trip.

1908   The Children's Act in Britain sets up special courts for young people.

1914-1918   The First World War.

1926   Television is invented — it won't be long before someone's blaming it for making kids go bad.

1932   Several kids get sent to prison — for going for a ramble in the countryside!

1939   The Second World War starts. By this time, all German children aged ten to eighteen have to be members of the Hitler Youth.

1949   American researcher William Sheldon blames muscly kids for all the crime.

1953   DNA is discovered. Later on, it'll be used to catch criminals.

1956   The American film Rock Around the Clock starts a wave of teenage riots in British cinemas.

1960s   Kid gangs run amok in Glasgow.

1964   Mods and rockers spend their bank holidays scrapping in Clacton, Margate and Brighton. Did someone start it by jumping on a sandcastle?

1965   The death penalty is abolished in Britain.

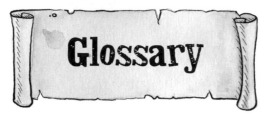

Glossary

Brat – bad kid

Bully – bad kid

Delinquent – bad kid

Enfant terrible – French for bad kid

Good-for-nothing – bad kid

Handful – bad kid

Hoodlum – bad kid

Hoody – bad kid

Hooligan – Irish for bad kid

Knave – bad kid

Larrikin – Australian for bad kid

Little devil – bad kid

Little monkey – bad kid

Minx – bad kid

Mischief-maker – bad kid

Miscreant – a very old French word for bad kid – from the Old French meaning 'unbeliever' – someone who behaves badly because they don't believe in God!

Ne'er-do-well – bad kid

Nuisance – bad kid

Oik – posh word for bad kid

Outlaw – bad kid

Pain in the neck – bad kid

Pesky kid – bad kid

Pest – bad kid

Ragamuffin – bad kid

Rapscallion – bad kid

Rascal – army word for bad kid

Reprobate – bad kid

Rogue – bad kid

Ruffian – bad kid

Scally – bad kid

Scallywag – American word for bad kid

Scamp – bad kid

Scoundrel – bad kid

Sinner – bad kid

Thug – bad kid

Troublemaker – bad kid

Tyke – bad kid

Urchin – from an old word for hedgehog. Later it meant a goblin who looked like a hedgehog. Now it means bad kid.

Varmint – bad kid

Villain – bad kid

Wastrel – bad kid

Whelp – bad kid

Whippersnapper – bad kid

Yob – bad kid or 'boy' backwards.

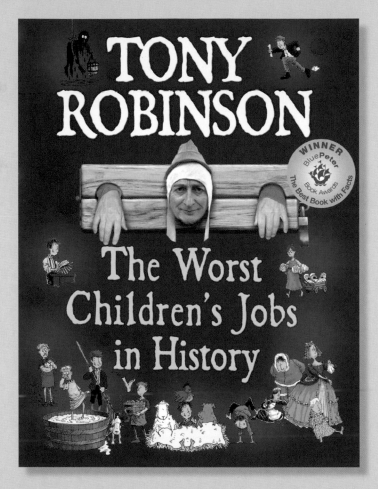

Next time you find yourself having to listen to your parents, grandparents, uncles, neighbours and random old people in the supermarket telling you how much harder they had it in their day, ask them if they were a jigger-turner or a turnip-picker. No? A mudlark perhaps? A stepper? Maybe they spent their weekends making matchboxes? Still no? Then they have no idea about the real meaning of hard work.

Tony Robinson takes you on a guided tour through all the lousiest places for a kid to work. With profiles and testimonies of real kids in rotten jobs, this book will tell you things you probably didn't want to know about the back-breaking, puke-inducing bits of being a child in the past.

The Worst Children's Jobs in History
ISBN 978-0-330-44286-4 £6.99

'Tony Robinson has written a book that will amuse and inspire even the most reluctant of historians'
TES

'. . . readers will find its blend of gruesome facts and dark humour irresistible . . . fascinating and horrifying reading'
Scotsman

'Kids will love the all-round ghastliness of this history lesson'
Belfast Telegraph

'Salutary food for thought for today's disenchanted youth'
Bookseller